PRAISE FOR *FRAGMENTS OF ISABELLA*

"This is one of the ever-glowing gems of the Holocaust experience." —Meyer Levin, author of *Compulsion*

"Profoundly moving . . . Leitner writes with a searing sensitivity that can move one to tears. Her slim volume is a celebration of the strength of the human spirit as it passes through fire." —*Publishers Weekly*

"A luminous and moving work, and an invaluable addition to the literature of history's most terrible tragedy . . . A voice not of defeat, but of affirmation." —Gerald Green, author of *Holocaust*

"Commands immediate nonstop reading. [Leitner] writes sparely, hauntingly, about very specific details—faces, voices, in a way that renders the unbearable real. . . . She breaks my heart open." —Phyllis Chesler, author of *Women and Madness*

"Isabella Leitner has helped to teach a new generation that we must not forget the past. She has done this in a moving and truthful way." —Elizabeth Swados

FRAGMENTS
OF ISABELLA

FRAGMENTS OF ISABELLA

— A Memoir of Auschwitz —

ISABELLA LEITNER

OPEN ROAD

INTEGRATED MEDIA

NEW YORK

Copyright © 1978 by Isabella Leitner and Irving A. Leitner

Cover design by Mauricio Díaz

ISBN: 978-1-5040-4935-1

This edition published in 2018 by Open Road Integrated Media, Inc.
180 Maiden Lane
New York, NY 10038
www.openroadmedia.com

The recall was painful.
My husband tiptoed around
me with deep, delicate concern.
This book belongs to him.

Isabella

CONTENTS

CONTENTS

FRAGMENTS
OF ISABELLA

You don't die of anything
except death.
Suffering doesn't kill you.
Only death.

NEW YORK, MAY 1945

Yesterday, what happened yesterday? Did you go to the movies? Did you have a date? What did he say? That he loves you? Did you see the new Garbo film? She was wearing a stunning cape. Her hair, I thought, was completely different and very becoming. Have you seen it? No? I haven't. Yesterday . . . yesterday, May 29, 1944, we were deported. . . .

Are the American girls really going to the movies? Do they have dates? Men tell them they love them, true or not. Their hair is long and blonde, high in the front and low in the back, like this and like that, and they are beautiful and ugly. Their clothes are light in the summer and they wear fur in the winter—they mustn't catch cold. They wear stockings, ride in automobiles, wear wristwatches and necklaces, and they are colorful and perfumed. They are healthy. They are living. Incredible!

Was it only a year ago? Or a century? . . . Our heads are shaved. We look like neither boys nor girls. We haven't menstruated for a long time. We have diarrhea. No, not diarrhea—typhus. Summer and winter we have but one type of clothing. Its name is "rag." Not an inch of it without a hole. Our shoulders are exposed. The rain is pouring on our skeletal bodies. The lice are having an orgy in our armpits, their favorite spots. Their bloodsucking, the irritation, their busy scurrying, give the illusion of warmth. We're hot at least under our armpits, while our bodies are shivering.

MAY 28, 1944–MORNING

It is Sunday, May 28th, my birthday, and I am celebrating, packing for the big journey, mumbling to myself with bitter laughter—tomorrow is deportation. The laughter is too bitter, the body too tired, the soul trying to still the infinite rage. My skull seems to be ripping apart, trying to organize, to comprehend what cannot be comprehended. Deportation? What is it like?

A youthful SS man, with the authority, might, and terror of the whole German army in his voice, has just informed us that we are to rise at 4 A.M. sharp for the journey. Anyone not up at 4 A.M. will get a *Kugel* (bullet).

A bullet simply for not getting up? What is happening here? The ghetto suddenly seems beautiful. I want to celebrate my birthday for all the days to come in this heaven. God, please let us stay here. Show us you are merciful. If my senses are accurate, this is the last paradise we will ever know. Please let us stay in this heavenly hell forever. Amen. We want nothing—nothing, just to stay in the ghetto. We are not crowded, we are not hungry, we are not miserable, we are happy. Dear ghetto, we love you; don't let us leave. We were wrong to complain, we never meant it.

We're tightly packed in the ghetto, but that must be a fine way to live in comparison to deportation. Did God take leave of his senses? Something terrible is coming. Or is it only me? Am I mad? There are seven of us in nine feet of space. Let them put fourteen together, twenty-eight. We will sleep on top of each other. We will get up at 3 A.M.—not 4—stand in line for ten hours. Anything. Anything. Just let our family stay together. Together we will endure death. Even life.

MAY 28, 1944–AFTERNOON

We are no longer being guarded only by the Hungarian gendarmes. That duty has been taken over by the SS, for tomorrow we are to be transported. From now on, the SS are to be the visible bosses.

Before this day, Admiral Horthy's gendarmes were the front men. Now they are what they always had been—the lackeys. Ever since childhood, I remembered them with terror in my heart. They were brutal, vicious—and anti-Semitic. Ordinary policemen, by comparison, are gentle and kind. But now, for the first time, the SS are to take charge.

My mother looks at me, her birthday baby. My mother's face, her eyes, cannot be described. From here on she keeps smiling. Her smile is full of pain. She knows that for her there is nothing beyond this. And she keeps smiling at me, and I can't stand it. I am silently pleading with her: "Stop smiling." I gaze at her tenderly and smile back.

I would love to tell her that she should trust me, that I will live, endure. And she trusts me, but she doesn't trust the Germans. She keeps smiling, and it is driving me mad, because deep inside I know she knows. I keep hearing her oft-made comment: "Hitler will lose the war, but he'll win against the Jews."

And now an SS man is here, spick-and-span, with a dog, a silver pistol, and a whip. And he is all of sixteen years old. On his list appears the name of every Jew in the ghetto. The streets are bulging with Jews, because Kisvárda, a little town, has to accommodate all the Jews of the neighboring villages. The SS do not have to pluck out every Jew from every hamlet. That work has already been done by the gendarmes. The Jews are now here. All the SS have to do is to send them on their way to the ovens.

The Jews are lined up in the streets. And now the sixteen-year-old SS begins to read the names. Those called form a group opposite us. "Teresa Katz," he calls—my mother. She steps forward. My brother, my sisters, and I watch her closely. (My father is in America trying to obtain immigration papers for his wife and children, trying to save them before Hitler devours them.) My mother heads toward the group.

Now the SS man moves toward my mother. He raises his whip and, for no reason at all, lashes out at her.

Philip, my eighteen-year-old brother, the only man left in the family, starts to leap forward to tear the sixteen-year-old SS apart. And we, the sisters—don't we want to do the same?

But suddenly reality stares at us with all its madness. My mother's blood will flow right here in front of our eyes. Philip will be butchered. We are unarmed, untrained. We are children. Our weapon might be a shoelace or a belt. Besides, we don't know how to kill. The SS whistle will bring forth all the other SS and gendarmes, and they will not be merciful enough to kill the entire ghetto—only enough to create a pool of blood. All of this flashes before us with crystal clarity. Our mother's blood must not be shed right here, right now, in front of our very eyes. Our brother must not be butchered.

And so my sister Chicha and I, standing next to Philip, step on his feet and hold his arms as hard as we can. And Philip's eyes flash in disbelief. We are all anguished. But we are all still alive.

MY FATHER

My father left Hungary for America. He left in trepidation, leaving his wife and six children behind. He left so he might save his family. He spent all his energies, all his love, banging on the doors of the authorities: "Give me immigration papers for my precious seven, so they can come here and live. Don't let them be murdered."

And they gave him the papers, *finally*.

But the clock ticked faster than the hands of bureaucracy moved. We received the necessary documents with instructions to be at the American consulate in Budapest on a certain Monday morning. My mother, Chicha, and I arrived in Budapest on Sunday. We were good and early, for on Monday morning we had an appointment with life!

We were at a friend's house, chatting happily about the

appointment, listening to music on the radio. There was a sudden interruption. The music stopped.

There was no appointment at the American consulate on Monday morning. It was December 8, 1941. Hungary had declared war against the United States.

The desperate father is again banging on the doors of the authorities: "Give me papers for Israel, so that my precious seven might live."

And they gave him the papers, *finally*.

And we received them . . . four weeks after Hitler had occupied Hungary. They could be framed . . . or used for toilet paper. I don't remember what we did with them.

Many years later, as you lay dying, Father, were you still tormented? Did you still think you had not done everything possible?

You tried, Father. You tried.

MAIN STREET, HUNGARY

Kisvárda was a small town in Hungary with a population of only 20,000. Yet it stands out in my memory as a very sophisticated "city" with visiting opera and theater companies, masquerade balls for the rich, cafés in which to while away the time trying to sound clever and worldly, auto racing, and horse racing. Barons, princes, and rich landowners, with their high-class manners and designer clothes, pranced around town in their fancy carriages. These aristocrats put their stamp on the town.

Main Street in Kisvárda (St. Laszlo Utca), I remember, smelled of French perfumes when I used to accompany my mother to the marketplace. The aroma would fill my nostrils as I'd watch my mother feel the force-fed geese to see if they were fat enough to nourish her six growing children—her bright, handsome, sensitive kids who would one day go out into the world well prepared by a mother whose intelligence and enlightenment were legendary and whose social conscience earned her my title "the poor man's Mrs. Roosevelt."

An avid reader, my mother marched her six kids off to the library every Friday to borrow the maximum number of books allowed to us, which she herself would devour before they had to be returned. And when my mother would buy fish for the Sabbath or holidays, she was incapable of throwing away the newspapers the fish were wrapped in before reading the smelly sheets first.

And I remember Teca, the gypsy, who used to come around to cast her sad eyes at my mother every day. Her source of sadness was always the same: "My children are hungry, Ma'am." And "Ma'am" would invariably fill Teca's potato sack with whatever she could spare. And anyone happening by at mealtime would automatically be invited to dine with us. "There will be enough. I'll put a little more water in the soup."

But mostly I remember the conversations my mother used to have with the many adults who came to visit us from other parts of Europe—business people, friends, relatives. The six kids stood around drinking in those very big words, those very big subjects—politics, art, books, and always *man's inhumanity to man*. Sometimes I was resentful. Must she care about everyone in this world? Look at me! Praise me! I want to be the most important! Why do you care so much about so many things?

But now, so many years later, I say: Thank you, Mother, for being what you were, for trying to develop me in every way.

Kisvàrda was just a little town. It's where I began, where I yearned to be away from. I didn't think I could take a large enough breath there. Yet the memories of my teens are crowded not only with teen pains but also with precious hours spent with dear friends in a house so alive with interests, thoughts, activities, conversations, dancing, playing, and falling in and out of love that my house—the whole town— seemed to be bursting apart.

But there were other things, too—bad things. I cannot count the times I was called a "dirty Jew" while strolling down Main Street, Hungary. Sneaky whispers: "Dirty Jew." No, "Smelly Jew"—that's what I heard even more often. Anti-Semitism, ever since I can remember, was the crude reality. It was always present in the fabric of life. It was probably so everywhere, we thought, but surely so in Hungary—most certainly in Kisvárda.

They really hate us, I would think. It certainly felt that way. You couldn't hide from it. You couldn't run from it. It was everywhere. It was thinly veiled, when it was veiled at all. It was just under the skin. It was hard to live with. But we did. We knew no other way.

Each "Heil Hitler!" speech on the radio made things worse. And such speeches were on the radio constantly. Not many people understood German in my part of Hungary, but the radio was blasting away Hitler's speeches, and the frenzy of the incessant "Heil Hitlers!" made the Hungarian gentiles feel a camaraderie, a oneness, with the mad orator. It also made us Jews cringe in the very depths of our souls. It made us fear the people with whom we had shared this town for generations.

What could we do?

Give us a patch of earth that is free of anti-Semitism!

We were afraid. Our neighbors, we knew, would be Hitler's willing accomplices when the bell would toll. And the bell tolled.

On Monday morning, May 29, 1944, the ghetto was evacuated. Jews, thousands upon thousands of Jews—every shape and form, every age, with every ailment, those whose Aryan blood was not Aryan enough, those who had changed their religion, oh, so long ago—dragged themselves down the main street toward the railroad station for what the Germans called "deportation." Upon their backs, bundles and backpacks—the compulsory "50 kilos of your best clothing and food" (which the Germans could later confiscate in one simple operation).

And the Hungarian townspeople, the gentiles—they were there too. They stood lining the streets, many of them smiling, some hiding their smiles. Not a tear. Not a good-bye. They were the good people, the happy people. They were the Aryans.

"We are rid of them, those smelly Jews," their faces read. "The town is ours!"

Main Street, Hungary.

A NEW MODE OF TRAVEL

We drag ourselves to the railroad station. The sun is mercilessly hot. People are fainting, babies screaming. We, the young and healthy teen-agers, are totally spent. What must the old, the sick, feel? Totally stripped of our dignity, leaving the town we were born in, grew up in—what happens after this long wait? Where are we off to?

I am ready to go. Away from my cradle of love. Away from where every pebble and every face are familiar. Those familiar faces now reflect gladness. I must be away before I learn to hate them. I shall not return.

You, my former neighbors, I cannot live with you again. You could have thrown a morsel of sadness our way while we were dragging ourselves down Main Street. But you didn't. Why?

Please take me away from here. I don't know these people.

I don't ever want to know them. I can't detect the difference between them and the SS, so I'll go with the SS.

Soon we are packed into the cattle cars . . . cars with barred windows, with planks of wood on the bars, so that no air can enter or escape . . . 75 to a car . . . no toilets . . . no doctors . . . no medication.

I am menstruating. There is no way for me to change my napkin . . . no room to sit . . . no room to stand . . . no air to breathe. This is no way to die. It offends even death. Yet people are dying all around me.

We squeeze my mother into a sitting position on the back-pack. Her face has an otherworldly look. She knows she will not live. But she wants us to live, desperately. All these years I've carried with me her face of resignation and hope and love:

"Stay alive, my darlings—all six of you. Out there, when it's all over, a world is waiting for you to give it all I gave you. Despite what you see here—and you are all young and impressionable—believe me, there is humanity out there, there is dignity. I will not share it with you, but it's there. And when this is over, you must add to it, because sometimes it is a little short, a little skimpy. With your lives, you can create other lives and nourish them. You can nourish your children's souls and minds, and teach them that man is capable of infinite glory. You must believe me. I cannot leave you with what you see here. I must leave you with what I see. My body is nearly dead, but my vision is throbbing with life—even here. I want you to live for the very life that is yours. And wherever I'll be, in some mysterious way, my love will overcome my death and will keep you alive. I love you."

And that frail woman of love lived until Wednesday.

THE ARRIVAL

We have arrived. We have arrived where? Where are we?

Young men in striped prison suits are rushing about, emptying the cattle cars. "Out! Out! Everybody out! Fast! Fast!"

The Germans were always in such a hurry. Death__ was__ always__ urgent__ with__ them—Jewish death. The earth had to be cleansed of Jews. We already knew that. We just didn't know that sharing the planet for another minute was more than this super-race could live with. The air for them was befouled by Jewish breath, and they must have fresh air.

The men in the prison suits were part of the Sonderkommandos, the people whose assignment was death, who filled the ovens with the bodies of human beings, Jews who were stripped naked, given soap, and led into the showers, showers of death, the gas chambers.

We are being rushed out of the cattle cars. Chicha and I are desperately searching for our cigarettes. We cannot find them.

"What are you looking for, pretty girls? Cigarettes? You won't need them. Tomorrow you will be sorry you were ever born."

What did he mean by that? Could there be something worse than the cattle-car ride? There can't be. No one can devise something even more foul. They're just scaring us. But we cannot have our cigarettes, and we have wasted precious moments. We have to push and run to catch up with the rest of the family. We have just spotted the back of my mother's head when Mengele, the notorious Dr. Josef Mengele, points to my sister and me and says, "*Die zwei.*" This trim, very good-looking German, with a flick of his thumb and a whistle, is selecting who is to live and who is to die.

Suddenly we are standing on the "life" side. Mengele has selected us to live. *But I have to catch up with my mother.*

Where are they going?

Mama! Turn around. I must see you before you go to wherever you are going. Mama, turn around. You've got to. We have to say good-bye. Mama! If you don't turn around I'll run after you. But they won't let me. I must stay on the "life" side.

Mama!

MY POTYO, MY SISTER

How could I have ever loved this much?

I had permission to bathe her. To diaper her. To burp her. To rock her. To love her.

She was "my" baby.

She would be a middle-aged woman now, and I still can't deal with having lost her.

The day we arrived in Auschwitz, there were so many people to be burned that the four crematoriums couldn't handle the task. So the Germans built big open fires to throw the children in. Alive? I do not know. I saw the flames. I heard the shrieks.

Is that the way you died, Potyo? Is that the way?

GRAVE

Life denied us the grace of a grave. Just a grave for my mother, my sister, my other sister. Just a grave to bring flowers to.

Is a Jew that low that a Jew cannot even have a grave? Even death is too good for a Jew?

I am not sentimental. I am not conventional. Yet I crave so a small piece of earth, a testimony that I too had a mother, that this planet is mine too, so the salt of my tears on that little mound might make me part of the whole scheme of things.

The smoke has vanished, and only I remember it. And nothing marks that noble mother but my heart.

You beast! Give me the body, that frail little body. I want to bury it.

"EAT SHIT"

It is just getting dark. We have been in Auschwitz for several hours. My mother has been dead for several hours. Little, dearest Potyo, too. It is Wednesday, May 31, 1944.

We are in this huge wet place. Thousands of us. They call it the showers. They call it disinfection, whatever that means. The SS are all around. Orders are being shrieked in a language we hardly understand, presumably German. The words sound like *"Louse! Louse! Louse!"* It seems to mean *"Rush! Rush! Rush!"*

We are being shoved, pushed, lined up. Some girls are working away in a fury. Only the work is unbelievable. We have never seen anything like it before. They are shaving the heads of the new arrivals. And their pubic hair. And their underarms. The furious speed is unbelievable. What they are doing is unbelievable. Within seconds, Chicha is somebody else. Some naked-headed monster is standing next to me. Some naked-headed monster is standing next to her.

That's all there is? The two of us? A few hours ago we were a large family. Where is everybody?

There is someone over there in that big crowd. She looks familiar. That shaved thing is someone Chicha and I seem to know. And next to her there is another. She looks familiar too. They are staring at us as well. We must know them. But we can't recognize them because they look so awful.

We inch toward each other. Is that you? Is that you? It's Rachel. It's Cipi. They are our sisters. There are four of us.

What happened? What happened, darlings? There are four of us. We are a big family. We just found two sisters. They just found us. My God, we are so happy!

What happened? That German who whistled while pointing some people to the left and some people to the right turned us all around in front of some horribly smoky place and made another selection. He took us out of the group, and they brought us here, and now there are four of us. We are so happy, and we look so terrible. What did they do to us, and where are we? What is going to happen?

Suddenly, in the midst of this chaos, this insanity, somebody steps through the window of our building and recognizes us, these four naked-headed monsters. He shakes our shoulders, tears rolling down his face. "Listen to me. Listen!

Eat whatever they give you. Eat. If they give you shit, eat shit. Because we must survive. We have to pay them back!"

And within seconds, my brother disappears through the window.

PHILIP

Philip, the caring Philip, the involved Philip, who managed to become some sort of ghetto official in Kisvárda so that at certain hours he would be permitted to leave the ghetto on "official" business. I don't know exactly what he did, but I do know that on the outside he would try to negotiate help for those on the inside.

Philip was overworked, exhausted, and every move he made was truly in the service of others. He was that kind of child, that kind of teen-ager. He is that kind of man. It is natural for Philip to be responsible to others. It was that way for my mother. Philip, more than any of us, is like my mother, whose heart truly was governed by the words "I am my brother's keeper." There are people like that. To be rendered totally helpless is probably more painful for such a person than for the rest of us.

Auschwitz lent itself to nothing. What could one do there to be a socially conscious human being? What could one do there to be a human being at all? With all odds against him, Philip found a way. He devised a means of communication. He was in a men's *Lager* some distance away, separated from us, as each *Lager* was, by electrified barbed-wire fences. One touch meant electrocution.

Somehow Philip acquired a knife. He found pieces of wood and began to carve messages: "My four sisters are in Lager C. Their name is Katz. Whoever finds this piece of wood, please keep tossing it over the fences until it reaches Lager C." And miraculously, the messages always reached us. Daily, the "mailmen" of Auschwitz, an unbroken chain of sufferers, would deliver the wood communication. Daily, at approximately the same spot, at approximately the same time, we would be standing there waiting for our "mail" from our ingenious brother, from the keeper of our souls. And the communication would always bear the same message: "You must survive. You must live. You simply must. We not only have to pay them back. That is not reason enough. We must build a future free of bloodshedding."

And though on planet Auschwitz, one was reduced to being an animal, Philip, your wooden gifts might have contributed to our survival. They just might have. So thank you, Philip.

Three weeks of wood blessings gave us a feeling of very special comfort, and we began to rely on those inanimate rechargers of our weakening spirit. Then the messages stopped. We stood at the usual spot for endless hours, endless days and weeks. We refused to accept the real message. Philip is no longer with us. He has left us. His legacy is lodged somewhere in our tortured hearts, but his body is gone—up in smoke, or where?

In 1945, when we were already in America, the mailman in New York bore a letter from an American soldier in Germany to my father. The soldier told us that he had liberated Philip but that Philip had a bullet wound in his leg. Philip was now in a hospital. He had survived six concentration camps, and he would be with us when he recovered.

Bless you, soldier.

Bless you, Philip, keeper of our souls, brother of man.

THE BABY

Most of us are born to live—to die, but to live first. You, dear darling, you are being born only to die. How good of you to come before roll call though, so your mother does not have to stand at attention while you are being born. Dropping out of the womb onto the ground with your mother's thighs shielding you like wings of angels is an infinitely nicer way to die than being fed into the gas chamber. But we are not having *Zeilappell*, so we can stand around and listen to your mother's muffled cries.

And now that you are born, your mother begs to see you, to hold you. But we know that if we give you to her, there will be a struggle to take you away again, so we cannot let her see you because you don't belong to her. You belong to the gas chamber. Your mother has no rights. She only brought forth fodder for the gas chamber. She is not a mother. She is just a dirty Jew who has soiled the Aryan landscape with another dirty Jew. How dare she think of you in human terms?

And so, dear baby, you are on your way to heaven to meet a recent arrival who is blowing a loving kiss to you through the smoke, a dear friend, your maker—your father.

CASTING IN AUSCHWITZ

It is a beautiful sunny Sunday. Summertime in Auschwitz. The crematoriums are taking a well-deserved rest. An easing of tension is hovering in the air. The sun must be healing our souls, burning out the pain from deep inside. There is something just a little bit different. They are leaving us alone a bit. The constant regimenting seems somewhat eased. What is it? Why? For whatever reason, it feels so good.

The little redheaded *Kapo* is busily scurrying about, asking all kinds of questions—who can sing what, play what instrument, recite what poem—the instant casting director. There will be a concert this afternoon in the *Lagerstrasse* for all to enjoy—the most unlikely cultural event on the face of the earth.

Rachel, known for her magnificent dramatic power in reciting poetry, is chosen. She can fuse heaven and hell when she recites the words "At the sight of this, even the mute will speak." And there is a cello, a violin, a flute. The musicians play sitting on chairs. (Chairs? We haven't seen one since we left home.) Thousands of people are sitting on the ground, in the sun, incredulously soaking in the sounds.

What does this all mean? Will there be a change? Have the Germans suddenly realized that we too have souls to be fed? Will they also feed our bodies? What does this all mean? Is this true? Or are we insane? Have they really succeeded and are we seeing imaginary things, hearing imaginary sounds in our tortured heads, sounds we vaguely remember to have loved? Please, somebody, tell us what is happening.

And somebody—or, rather, something—does. Airplanes are flying over our heads. The Germans are taking pictures of the humane treatment we are receiving in the legendary Auschwitz. The world will soon have proof of Germany's humanity to men.

MUSULMANS

Selections. Selections. Selections. To weed out the *Musulmans*. To be a lone person in Lager C was perhaps a blessing. To have sisters still alive, not to be alone, was a blessing too, but fraught with tests daily, hourly: When this day ends, will there still be four of us?

If you are sisterless, you do not have the pressure, the absolute responsibility to end the day alive. How many times did that responsibility keep us alive? I cannot tell. I can only say that many times when I was caught in a selection, I knew I had to get back to my sisters, even when I was too tired to fight my way back, when going the way of the smoke would have been easier, when I wanted to, when it almost seemed desirable. But at those times, I knew also that my sisters, aware that I was caught up in a selection, not only wanted me to get back to them—they expected me to get back. The burden to live up to that expectation was mine, and it was awesome.

Does staying alive not only for yourself, but also because someone else expects you to, double the life force? Perhaps. Perhaps.

Rachel, more vulnerable than the rest of us, pleaded with us, oh, so often. "If I'm separated from you, if they should take me on transport, don't count on me. Alone, I won't make it. I don't want to make it. Whatever effort I am making now is all for you. I no longer care to live—unless, and only if, we are together. The minute we're separated, I'll be on my way to the crematorium, and that will be fine with me. You are forcing me to stay alive, and I'm so tired."

Rachel hardly slept—much less so than the rest of us. The terror of being separated kept her awake. Only the terror of separation, not fear of death. We pleaded with her incessantly to promise to fight for her life should we be separated. She pleaded with us incessantly not to ask this much.

The responsibility of staying alive had its own inherent torture. At times it doubled the alertness, at times I wished I were alone, not to be asked to go constantly, on a twenty-four-hour basis, against the tide. After all, the business of Auschwitz was death. It is not everywhere that death is so easily to be gotten.

I am tired. Let me go. . . . No, we won't. Our business is life.

My darling sisters, you are asking too much. And I am

asking too much of you. Yet the insanity of Auschwitz must be imbued with meaning if *living* is to be continued, and the only meaning to living has to be for the four of us to be where the sun shines, or the smoke blackens the sky. All of us. Together.

Chicha was working in the *Unterkunft*. Some of the 50 kilos of belongings that we lugged on our backs the day they dragged us to the railroad station for deportation were sorted out in the *Unterkunft*. That is where Chicha's tears poured on my brother's pajamas when she recognized the patch my mother had sewn on them. The *Unterkunft* was one of the few places where so-called work was performed in Lager C. Lager C was a *Vernichtungslager*, an annihilation *Lager*. The Germans kept us there not for work, but to become *Musulmans*, crematorium fodder.

Have you ever seen a *Musulman*? Have you ever weighed 120 pounds and gone down to 40? Something like that—not quite alive, yet not quite dead. Can anyone, can even I, now picture it?

The *Unterkunft* was a place where on a few occasions you could go undetected while stealing something—the word for it was "organizing"—and the occasions when one could organize were very, very few. But Chicha once brought out a knife hidden in her shoes, and when we sliced our bread (Was it really bread? It tasted like sawdust) into paper-thin miracles, we were able to delude ourselves that we had a lot of food, that our daily ration was really bigger than we thought.

Of course, the delusion lasted only a little while. The incredible hunger quickly reminded us of the lie. But lie we did. In our minds it was one more act of defiance. *"You see, Hitler, we are smarter than you. This will keep* Musulman*ship away from us."*

Hell, no, it didn't. Our eyes sank deeper. Our skin rotted. Our bones screamed out of our bodies. Indeed, there was barely a body to house the mind, yet the mind was still working, sending out the messages *"Live! Live!"*

On this day the SS invaded Block 10 through both the front and back entrances of the barracks. At other times, they would surprise us by coming in through only one entrance. That left a possibility of slipping out the other, escaping the selection—a slim possibility, but still some were able to slip out to the *Lagerstrasse* and be relatively safe until the next selection. After all, an hour of life is an hour of life. Why not make a run for it? It became a way of life, a way of death postponement.

Not this day. On this day Mengele came with his air of superiority to exercise his superior judgment with his right thumb and his left thumb: *This is a Musulman. This is not— not yet.* He did this with an air of elegance. Cool and elegant. Yes, that was Mengele.

Caught in the trap, we were all hysterical—1,000 prisoners

locked hopelessly in Block 10. The whole SS operation had taken but a few minutes.

Suddenly, with an awesome life instinct, Cipi, Rachel, and I began to mimic the *Stubendiensts*, the Jewish *Kapos*, in their screaming, so as to appear to be one of them and thus escape the selection. Chicha, working in the *Unterkunft*, by now must know that Mengele is in Block 10. We must get out of here, we thought, back to her. Also, once again, we must survive. And so we screamed with an air of importance, as if we had assigned duties, as if we belonged to the wretched leadership. We screamed incoherently. We looked important. "Move! Don't move! This way! That way!" Anything, so long as we could convince the SS that we were working in Block 10, that we were aiding the beast. Our struggle for survival was now keener than at any other time. The seconds that separated us from death overwhelmed us with a reality we had never felt with any other selection. Both doors were bolted. Escape was impossible. But we could not be selected to die. We had to remain in Block 10 with those chosen to live. In the past, after the selection, the *Musulmans* had always been led away to the oven. That was the way it was always done. That's why we had to stay behind.

But now came the Nazis' evil ingenuity. This time, they reversed their procedure. This time, they led a group of prisoners out as usual, but now, after our insane struggle to remain behind, as we looked around, we found ourselves surrounded not by the so-called healthy ones, but by the *Musulmans*, the crematorium fodder.

No! No! No! We won't go to the crematorium. Not yet. Not now. With nothing to lose but our lives, Cipi, Rachel, and I rushed to one of the two bolted doors now being guarded by an emaciated inmate. With a power that emanates not from the body but from the spirit, we charged forward. The skeletal guard stepped out of our way, and we crashed against the door. The bolt snapped. The door gave way. And we were outside in the *Lagerstrasse*.

And there—fully expecting us, I am sure—was Chicha.

"Chicha, Chicha! Don't cry!"

IRMA GRESE AND CHICHA

Is the face a mirror? Is that mirror incapable of recording so much cruelty that it makes a complete turnabout and records beauty instead? How else could Irma Grese have been so perfectly beautiful? Flawless skin. A head of natural blond hair. Almost perfect features. Who made this beautiful beast? Who was responsible for this mockery?

Irma Grese—dressed in immaculate SS uniform, usually with a light-blue shirt, a silver pistol in her holster, a huge dog at her side. The beautiful monster, our *Oberscharführerin*, our twice daily visitor, trailing her merciless terror behind her. Bisexual.

It is said that Chicha appeals to her. This manifests itself only in the fact that she always recognizes her and either tortures her more than the others or (on one occasion) does not send her off to die. This was the extent of her lesbian behavior toward Chicha. But torture her she did, in a fiendish manner, one particular afternoon.

Lager C, our *Lager*, was designed to hold 30,000 prisoners, 1,000 in each block (barracks). On this late summer afternoon, the 30,000 prisoners, in rows of five, were once again being counted—*Zeilappell*, they called it—and Grese was doing the counting. This was often a sham, with the SS claiming that a prisoner was missing, and therefore we would have to stand upright in line until every single prisoner was accounted for. Indeed, the SS needed no excuses, and certainly, no one had ever escaped, but the device must have amused them, so frequently did they resort to it.

Now, as Grese counted, she came not from the *Lagerstrasse*—where we could see her approaching and thus ready ourselves to stand up straight—but instead from behind the blocks. Such surprises always worked in favor of the SS and left us more helpless than before. At the rear of a column of *Fünferreihe* (rows of five prisoners), a girl was sitting on the ground to gather enough strength to stand erect for the moment that Grese would appear.

At *Zeilappell*, all prisoners must stand erect for whatever number of hours the roll call lasts. It is one of the sacred rituals. Any deviation is a mortal sin. In retrospect, it seems to me that not standing erect was a subtle sign of the spirit ebbing away, the readiness to be off to the *Kremchy* (the crematorium.) This is, perhaps, too broad a generalization;

nonetheless, the conclusion is inescapable because the life force seems to have pushed us always to stand straight for just one more *Zeilappell*. I did not think of it then, but what, if not the life force, made me stand erect with a 104-degree fever, with typhus so severe that our dear emaciated doctor friend, a fellow prisoner, kept saying, "At home, with the best of care, you would have died long ago"?

The girl resting on the ground was caught in the act by Grese. But Grese attributed the "crime" not to the girl, but to Chicha. Grese's attraction to Chicha, as her whole life did, took an aberrant form. She yanked Chicha out of the line to punish her. She dragged her to the center of the *Lagerstrasse* for all to see how crime does not pay. She made her kneel, lifted Chicha's arms high in the air, and placed two heavy rocks in her hands. She then ordered Chicha to hold her arms straight up for the duration of the *Zeilappell*. *"And no wavering of the arms! If you do, you'll die! I'll return to check on you."* And so she did, over and over again, taunting Chicha, *"Have you had enough? Do you like it?"* She would touch Chicha's arms with her whip. *"They are not straight enough. There you go."*

Thousands of eyes stared at the bonelike creature in the *Lagerstrasse* seemingly holding two mountains, so frail did she look in comparison to the rocks. She, the rock herself—with all the prisoners' eyes turned heavenward in prayer: "God, do not let her drop the rocks, because then she'll die, and a little bit of our spirit, our determination to live and tell this tale, will die with her. God, help us to imbue her with out unified spirit, keep her arms straight, keep our souls riveted to hers, and maybe we'll all live. Do not desert us now. The hour that pits good against evil is right here, right now, on this ugly piece of land, mutilated by gas chambers and crematoriums that devour by the millions the highest form of life, each of which took nine months to cry out. They cry no more. Their silence deafens Chicha's ears. Their silence straightens Chicha's arms. The chorus of dead silently whisper in her soul, 'Keep your arms straight. Keep your arms straight. For the dead and for the living. For the dead and for the living.'"

A fury of thoughts rushed through our heads: *That human being out there on display in the* Lagerstrasse *is our sister. A halo is glowing around her shriveled body. Her strength is being tested ferociously. Her three sisters' strength is being tested ferociously, too. Will she make it? How much longer can we endure her endurance? Trust me! Trust us!*

The gentile woman from Budapest, she of noble birth, who was sent to Auschwitz because she had committed an unpardonable crime—she had helped her Jewish friends . . . I no longer remember her name, only her aristocratic face, drawn and hungry. She had been the fifth person in our *Fünferreihe*. She died in the ovens later, but now she was with us, and we loved her, and she loved us. There had not been any need for intellectual utterances for a long while now. Only the language of survival was of import here. Yet with her, on occasion, we actually talked of books. Strange must be the ways of the hungry, for even while the body is starving, the mind may crave nourishment too.

This gentile woman stood with us now as we watched Chicha, and her words will linger in my mind for all my days to come: "I had to save my friends. I just had to. Yet, through these months of suffering, I have thought of the luxurious ways of the privileged that I gave up. Yes, at times—ashamed as I am to say it—doubts, even regret, kept creeping into my head. But today"—and she took a long, compassionate look at Chicha—"I know with absolute certainty why I am here. This is where I belong. I could not be anywhere else. Guilt from a lavish life would tear my guts asunder while all of this is taking place around me. At this moment in history I belong here, with you, with the innocent, with Chicha, with her arms raised toward the heavens. I belong standing next to the three of you, caressing your wounded hearts, and I tell you with absolute certainty that she will make it."

As we stood there in our columns, endless hours passed. At last, Grese returned. She strode up to Chicha. She knew she had been defeated. "Put those rocks down," she said.

RACHEL

It is now October 1944, six months after we arrived, and the four of us are still alive. We have avoided every single selection so far. But now it is Sunday morning, and there is a sudden selection—sudden, as always.

Rachel, our little sister, is too young, too broken in spirit and body. She will not possibly be able to make it. She is all too ready for the oven. But it cannot happen. We must keep her alive. We love her too dearly.

Mengele is selecting a little distance away from us. He is selecting the *Musulmans*, those who are totally emaciated, those who have no possibility of being chosen for work transport. He is selecting for the oven.

Suddenly, frantically, we try to make Rachel healthier looking, older looking (she is only fifteen and a half). Mengele must not have his way. We will keep her alive.

One of us has a piece of cloth. We place it on Rachel's head as a kerchief. We make her stand on tiptoes while she pleads that she has no strength for such superhuman efforts. We pinch her face to an unnatural redness . . .

Mengele passes her by.

This day the crematorium has been cheated of our precious sister. This day Hitler has lost and we have won—wit against might. We will live on for another day.

SERENITY

Yes, six months in Auschwitz. And the four of us are still alive. And we are together—the single most important thing. We touch each other. Cipi, Chicha, Rachel, Isabella—the four sisters together, and we seem to be alive. Dazed, weighing probably no more than 40, 50, 60 pounds each, but words come out of our lips, so we must be alive. In sort of an otherworldly way.

We don't look like anything we have ever seen, but on the other hand, we no longer know what anything looks like. Or anyone. We live among *Musulmans*. The whole world must be populated with *Musulmans*. The Germans look like things we have seen before. They have ruddy cheeks, immaculate uniforms, but the sickness of their souls and the stench of death about them are so pervasive that we are not sure they are real.

We are pure and beautiful. We have nothing in common with them. They are Germans. We were born of mothers the smell of whose burning flesh permeates the air, but what were they born of? Who sired them?

The little baby born yesterday, whose mother remained alive because her pregnancy was not noticed, is off now to the crematorium. She was born only to die immediately. What was your hurry, lit-the baby? Couldn't you have waited until the house painter was dead, so you could have lived? Couldn't the gods have arranged for a longer pregnancy so that evil, not life, would be murdered? For a moment, for just a moment, we had a real smell of a real life, and we touched the dear little one before she was wrapped in a piece of paper and quickly handed to the *Blockelteste* so the SS wouldn't discover who the mother was, because then she, too, would have had to accompany the baby to the ovens. That touch was so delicious. Are we ever to know what life-giving feels like? Not here. Perhaps out there, where they have diapers, and formulas, and baby carriages—and life.

And now it was November 1944. The business of Auschwitz had to be terminated because soon the Russians would march in, and the Germans were thinking: *Let's ship some of these* Musulmans *on work transport and send the rest to the crematorium. Let's wrap up this whole Auschwitz business.*

Not many were left in Lager C, my *Lebensraum* for the past six months. They rounded us up. To go where? To the work transport? To the ovens? Which would it be? Does it matter? The four of us are together—that is what matters.

And they led us away from this heaven. I say "heaven" because, so far, each change we have gone through was for the worse. Perhaps the next one would make us long for what we have now. And yes, they took us to the crematorium.

We stood there all night, the smoke furiously spewing out of the stacks, bringing with it an illusion of warmth in the dread, cold November night. And the serenity we felt, we will never forget. We had made it all the way here together. We cheated them out of the joy of tearing us in four different directions. For a lone person, it didn't matter which way you went—you left no one behind. When it was possible to save four members of the same family, the only thing that mattered was that you all went the same way. We are doing that now. This is the last stop. Nothing can change this. We are leaving no one behind. It is unalterable, but we feel a serenity that we never felt before. We are together and can face whatever follows the end of this long, silent, serene vigil. Together to the ovens. A note of thanks, bitchy Fate.

But then the end of this chilly November night came. And as had happened so many times before, the German orders were changed. This crematorium-bound group was ordered into an icy set of trains to be sent to another concentration camp.

'Bye, Auschwitz. I will never see you again. I will always see you.

BIRNBAUMEL

Auschwitz was behind us. Birnbaumel in eastern Germany was our new concentration camp home. It had a great advantage: It had no crematorium. It had a great advantage: It had no electrified fences that one could—as so many had done in Auschwitz—touch and die. The camp was at one end of the forest. The tank traps we dug were at the other end. To go from one to the other, we had to march through the town, twice a day, coming and going. In the morning, we were marched through the town, every day—a thousand watched young women. The pity of that sight could make a beast weep. But not the Germans.

Churchbells ringing. The smell of fresh bread from bakeries. Children going to school. The life of a small town. It was even a little bit like home. Then, toward evening, we were marched through the town again. But the Germans never saw us. Ask them. They never saw us. Come to think of it, they really didn't. It was beneath their Aryan dignity. We were just a lot of filthy Jews. Why even glance at us? In the comfort of their homes, they probably cast gentle loving gazes at their cats, or dogs, or whatever. They were sensitive. They were cultured. Germany was one giant concentration camp, with Jews marching the length and breadth of the country, but these refined, sensitive Germans never saw us. Find me a German who ever saw me. Find me one who ever harmed us.

It was December, and there was this fat *Oberscharführer*, whose flesh alone would have kept him warm. He was one of our guards, and he used to stand by the fire we built in the forest, warming his huge rump, while chasing us away from the fire with the butt of his rifle. The fire, indeed, was necessary. We couldn't dig the earth. It was frozen. It had to be heated up first. Keep the earth warm. Not the Jews.

In that forest, the fire of resistance kept my frozen body alive. My mother had told me not to aid my enemy. In that forest in Birnbaumel in December, I remembered her. I honored her and kept myself alive. The other inmates shoveled diligently as if they were building a castle for themselves, claiming that only by working very hard could they keep a semblance of warmth. True. Yet it was not. I begged some of them to sabotage the work, to pick up their shovels only when the Germans left the fire to make their rounds. They didn't, or couldn't, listen. While I could listen only to my inner voices, to the infallible truth my mother had taught me.

I was a one-woman sabotage team. As soon as the Germans walked away, I would put down my shovel and stop digging. Digging to me symbolized digging my own grave. In reality, that was what it was. And even in that place, I had self-respect to preserve. My emaciated body still housed a soul to be tended and cared for, and when I could nourish it, I did.

HITTING THE CELT

Birnbaumel could hardly inspire anything, yet for some reason, I noticed my own fractured humanness there. The first night we arrived in Birnbaumel, I overheard some of the *Oberscharführer*'s instructions to his fellow SS. They were to choose ten *Kapos* from among the prisoners—one for every 100 inmates. This was unlike Auschwitz, where there was one *Kapo* for every 1,000—not to mention the various ugly positions below the *Kapo*.

The German genius had, of course, variations of evil, one of which was to appoint torturers from among the inmates themselves. Brother against brother. Sister against sister. And if you survived long enough, you realized that the minutest advantage might help you make it through. In many cases the Germans realized their intentions. They succeeded in brutalizing some of us. But only some. Only some. A small number of people survived as much as five or six years. Dehumanization of such long duration can take a toll beyond all comprehension. I don't mean dehumanization only of the soul, but the simultaneous dehumanization of the body as well. The German hate-bombardment, the teaching of hatred to their own people, was directed only at their souls (if indeed there were souls there to begin with). The German bodies were well nurtured with the food Hitler stole from country after country. But we drank urine and ate sawdust. You can't do that for long and remain brave and human and upright.

So when the time came, I was there to be chosen to be a *Kapo*. If I learn how to be a *Kapo*, I reasoned, who knows, we might stay alive and be there to greet out liberators. I owe it to my sisters to try to keep all of us alive. Ah, dear God, teach me how to be a *Kapo*!

And I was chosen. I was a *Kapo*. And using my new authority, I was able to assign Rachel to be the toilet cleaner of the camp, Chicha to be the cleaner of our celt (an umbrella-like wooden barracks), and Cipi to be her assistant. All of this meant that they did not have to go out daily to dig in the forest and return with their legs frozen, as so many did.

One of my duties as *Kapo* was to round up those prisoners who tried to avoid going to the forest. This happened daily, and the SS woman in charge gave me a huge stick and showed me how to beat the runaways. Waving the stick in the air, I ran around the camp screaming orders as loud as I could. I tried to sound as brutal as possible, and I used the stick with as much might as I could muster. But at last I was caught by the SS. I was striking the walls of the celt, not the inmates. I simply couldn't . . . I *couldn't* hurt anyone. I fell from grace with a thud. I had been a *Kapo* for two days. I wasn't shot, but from then on I was always recognized as the ex-*Kapo* who could never escape the trip to the forest.

MY HEART IS BEATING

My heart is beating. Faster and faster. It will be me. The *Oberscharführer* will choose me. I know he will. Along with several others. To carry the dead girl to her grave. I can dig the grave, but please, please don't choose me to carry the body. Have mercy. I cannot carry the dead body. Inside, deep in my being, I am just a child. The dead, cold body I cannot touch. It makes me shiver. Please. Please.

There is no crematorium in which to burn the dead in Birnbaumel. The dead actually have to be buried, out some distance from the camp. It is done at night, in the ominous night, and I am frightened. So terribly frightened. Don't choose me.

But he does. And then the pitiful little band is off to the hill to perform the sacred mission. Chicha is chosen as a grave digger, and four others are chosen to carry the body.

We are off to a patch of earth in a foreign land that is soaked with the blood of the innocent, the young, the unfulfilled, the martyred children of martyred Jewish mothers who dared to give life in an age of death.

I am about to slip my trembling palms under the corpse when Chicha softly, compassionately, whispers in my ear: "I will put my hands under the body, and you put your hands on mine." Tears are rolling down my cheeks. Not for the dead girl, but for the goodness that is still alive, that refuses to be buried, however hard the madman tries to still the voice of God in man.

Rest in peace, young girl. The flickering stars above must be the weeping children of your womb. The womb, the glorious womb, the house that celebrates life, where life is alive, where the bodies of young girls are not carried out into the night. Rest in peace, young girl.

IN THE "HOSPITAL" AT BIRNBAUMEL

The daily trip to the forest took its toll. Both my spirit and my body hung on by less than a thread. Ill with typhus, I was finally put in the *Revere*, the concentration camp's version of a hospital, which resembled no hospital anyone has ever seen. You slept on the cold earth, you defecated right there, because you were no longer human enough to go out—and, of course, you were beaten for it.

The only advantage of being in the *Revere* was that you did not have to go out to the forest. You were lying mostly with people who could no longer walk, who were hopelessly ill with gangrene. The odor could drive you mad, but you no longer cared because there were only a few more days of life left in you, and death would be welcome.

My sisters came every night to pump spirit into my near-death body. "Please, please make yourself live. We held on this long—it really would be sacrilegious to give up now. You must hold out. The Nazis' end must be near." And "Here is a tiny piece of bread," said Chicha. "You mustn't think that I took it away from myself. I really, really am not hungry."

And they came every night to pump life into me. I am sure that I did not want to live. But every night, they were there, terror-stricken that the bone they called a sister was no longer alive.

But the bone had a heart that refused to stop beating. And the bone would greet the three sunken-eyed visitors.

JANUARY 22, 1945

We have left Birnbaumel. We are now in another German town. I think we are not far from Breslau. I think the town is Prauschnitz. That is how I remember it. It is Monday, January 22, 1945. It is the end of the workday. The town is rushing home. This time we are not marching through the center but are sort of mingling with the home-going townspeople. This time we aren't so painfully lined up by the SS guards, so terribly organized. This is very unlike the Germans. The system, it seems, is beginning to fall apart.

I have a curious, unreal feeling, one of almost being part of the grayish dusk of the town. But again, of course, you will not find a single German who lived in Prauschnitz who ever saw a single one of us. Still, we were there, hungry, in rags, our eyes screaming for food. And no one heard us. We ate the smell of smoked meats reaching our nostrils, blowing our way from the various shops. Please, our eyes screamed, give us the bone your dog has finished gnawing. Help us live. You wear coats and gloves just like human beings do. Aren't you human beings? What is underneath the coats? Who is mad? You? Or we? Somebody, please, tell us.

Suddenly, in the open sewer to my side, there is a funny-looking inmate scurrying for a hiding place. May God be with you. Escape is impossible, but may you be the one who succeeds. For the guts you have, you deserve it.

And yes, she succeeded. She was out of sight, undetected. But a moment later she was back. She had crawled back to the line of prisoners.

"I couldn't leave you. I can't live while you die. We must all escape or perish together." That scrawny, scurrying thing was my sister.

Dear Chicha, how much longer will our pact hold? Must we all die unless we all survive together? We must learn to break the bond. Therein lies life. Our pact must end, else none will be left. We must soon be liberated, or we will soon die, because there is only a little bit of life left in us. We must make a new pact—each for herself. We can no longer fight for each other as before. There simply isn't enough life left in us. We must seek whatever there can be for us, any change at all, alone if it has to be. Let us learn a new way of life, of death. Please, let each of us understand this. The old pact must go. A new one must take its place. Somebody will have to live. Somebody must. No argument about this. It is final. We cannot all die. Somebody will have to keep this sturdy gene alive. Somebody must live to tell the tale.

THE BARN

That night, we are at our new camp, evacuated the night before by the thousands who came before us. But there isn't enough room, and some of us are shoved into a barn. So here we are, the four of us, together with some other miserable creatures. As dawn approaches, we try to bury ourselves deep in the hay. Perhaps the SS will not find us when he pokes around with his pitchfork for those who stubbornly insist on surviving.

When we left the forest camp in Birnbaumel the day before to walk in the freezing snow toward Bergen-Belsen, we didn't realize that we were being rushed so desperately because the Russian army was close behind us. Indeed, the Russians were so close that had we hidden ourselves somewhere in Birnbaumel, the Germans would not have had the time to look for us and we would have been liberated by the

Russian army that very afternoon. But we didn't know that then. All we knew was that the Germans were in a hurry to take us farther west, and, if possible, we must not go. So now, in the barn, we dug ourselves deep into the hay.

When the Germans were ready to move on, sure enough, they had no time to go looking separately for each prisoner who tried to escape. But they were not about to let their Jews go so easily. They were too diabolical. So they began to cook potatoes. Soon the smell of food began to fill the air, and a moment later, the stubborn will to live that we had nourished for so long evaporated completely.

One by one we emerged from the haystack and staggered toward the food line. The smell of potatoes evidently was more powerful than the will to live. But by the time we reached the kettle, not a morsel was left.

Yes, the Germans were smarter than we—or, perhaps, not as hungry. Under those conditions, it was easy to play maddening games of death. The year 1945 was not the kind in which somebody could be smart. That time, that month, that day shames my soul now, because I no longer am hungry and I can't imagine how I could have sold my freedom for the smell of a potato.

The hay was all over. It was in our eyes, in our hair—it must have been mixed up with our brains. Yes, that's what it was, hay in the brains. How could we have imagined that we ever again would walk, talk, feel like human beings? We had tried to interfere with the work of the manufacturers of death, and you cannot do that. The Germans' bible was death, and humiliation, and dehumanization, and they succeeded so well that they destroyed our ability to reason, and we voluntarily leaped back into their arms. And so many decades later, it still hurts that the animals in those spick-and-span uniforms, in those shiny boots, had the cunning to lure us back to destruction by rubbing our noses in an aroma.

I curse you, even from the distance of these many years, for keeping me so hungry that it affected my brain and subordinated me to your evil. And my apologies to the animals for comparing you to them, because surely animals are more humane.

JANUARY 23, 1945

Back in the line, the pitiful thousand, minus the few who did escape, the many who died, we are on our way to walk the infinite distance to Bergen-Belsen. Our pact now is not spoken but fully understood. Any of the four sisters is now allowed (meant in a deep emotional sense) to vanish, to die, to give up, to live. The faintest possibility of aiding each other morally or physically no longer exists.

Eastern Germany is bitter cold in January. There is a blizzard. Rachel is coughing very badly. On one foot she has a torn leather shoe, on the other a Dutch wooden shoe. In the blizzard and with the uneven shoes, she can barely drag herself along. Between the four of us, we are missing one shoe, and whichever one tries to aid Rachel by giving up a shoe will be the one to die. In the past, we always found a solution—an abnormal solution in an abnormal setting, but still, some kind of solution. But we cannot crack this one. For one of us, death is hours away. What to do? Is the life force strong enough yet to make us act if there is another opportunity? Will instinct guide us to survival? We don't know.

We are marching in the blizzard in *Fünferreihe*. Always five in a row. For the four of us, this was a special problem because to be five in a row was the prisoners' responsibility. And so we always had to find an unattached girl for our row. And when we found one, it was never permanent, for sooner or later she died, was taken on transport or to the crematorium, or attached herself to someone else. It was a continuous struggle.

But now we are marching in the blizzard on a silent, deserted road. SS guards are in front, leading the column, on both sides, and in the rear. We have just reached a tiny village called Jagadschutz. Suddenly, Chicha notices a little house to her right. It is covered with snow, and no smoke is coming from the chimney. Chicha is on the outside of the column. Rachel is next to her. I am next to Rachel, and Cipi is next to me. The side guards have gone to the rear because some prisoners have escaped. Only the guards in the front remain, and they can't see us from their position.

In a flash, Chicha is running toward the house. Then Rachel. Then I. There is no thinking on our parts. Not a word among us. Just one sister following the other.

Rachel and I ran to a tiny doghouse behind the main house and crawl inside. Everything is totally silent, deserted. Deep snow blankets the area. The scene is reminiscent of Christmas—"Peace on earth, goodwill toward men."

Crouched in the doghouse, we are not breathing. There is nothing but silence and terror. When will they kill us? Where are they? Why did we escape?

Slowly, carefully, we inch our way out. We crouch behind the doghouse. Silence again. Where is Chicha? Where is Cipi? Silence. Only silence.

Suddenly there is the sound of crackling snow on the road. The *Oberscharführer*, with his dog, is coming back from the slaughter—we heard the shots. He is cursing the filthy Jews for slowing down the column by attempting to escape. He is utterly furious, mumbling to himself, in a hurry to catch up with the group. We can see him from our crouching position. He cannot see us.

But the dog will smell us. Rachel and I automatically grab our chests. What will it feel like—the bullet? Oh! Oh! Please, please don't do it. Will it be in the chest or in the head? Will it hurt terribly? Will we die immediately? If not, will he shoot again?

Till now we have seen only other people die, and it was awful. But this will be us. It will be me. Now we know we are only seconds away from death, and it is terrible. It would have been better if we hadn't seen him, if our backs were to him. Then we wouldn't have known in advance that we are going to be murdered. Cruel, ugly Fate. At least not to know, not to see him point the rifle at us.

God! God, help us! This once. You have not shown us any mercy all these months. Have mercy. My chest feels awful. Something will rip it apart in a second. Can't you do something, God? Don't let us die. Not this way. Not here. Not now. Not ever. Death, go away—go! Please!

I have lived barely two decades. Rachel is only 16. Will nobody help us? Will this dog and this dog of a man just rip us apart in a second? Somebody, please help us! Isn't there anybody in this whole world who cares? We haven't done anything. We have hardly lived. We have known barely anything but war.

Where is my mother? She will protect us. Mama! Where are you? Somebody is trying to kill your children. The *Oberscharführer* is coming to kill us. He is coming closer . . . closer. He is right here.

He is gone.

What happened? Was the wind blowing our scent away from the dog? We are not dead. There is no bullet in our chests. . . . We are alive. . . . He is gone.

THE HOUSE

"Isabella, Rachel, Cipi. Are you all here? Where are you? I am in the attic. I found a frozen cabbage, and it's delicious. Hurry, come up here; the house is empty; there's no one around. Are you all here?"

"No, Chicha, just the two of us—Rachel and Isabella. Cipi probably ran into the next house, or the one after that. She's here somewhere, and when it's all safe, we'll find her."

"Then come on up and let's eat, before the Germans come back to kill us. Let's eat."

We ran up to the attic. To Chicha. To the cabbage. To happiness.

Now, there was an ever so faint noise. We peered through a hole. The door downstairs was being opened with the very greatest caution. A terrified head could be seen looking around. Then another, and then a third.

With the voices of those whose death sentence has just been deferred, we cried out: "It is us! It is us!"

We ran downstairs, quite certain by now that the house was deserted, and hugged the three new arrivals, the three brave inmates who had also escaped. Cipi was not among them, but we were not worried. We were quite sure she was somewhere in the vicinity.

The people who had been living in the house must have been in an awful hurry to get away, for their milk had been left unrefrigerated and untouched. They had run in haste with their beloved Nazis toward western Germany. This little house was now ours, to do with as we liked.

And what did we like?

Food! And we found it. In abundance. A pantry filled with smoked meat. An entire pig. Greasy, smoked, awful, marvelous, fantastic, glorious—all ours, to be eaten instantly, all of it, this very second. And we did.

We ate and ate—not ate, devoured. Without a stop. Now the Nazis can do as they like. We have eaten. We are eating. And will eat until the second our lives are snuffed out. The only reason to live is to eat.

Oh, my stomach. It hurts. It deliciously hurts. It's filled. It cannot hold any more food. But that will not stop any of us. Eat. Eat.

There is no toilet indoors. We'll use that huge bin. We are alternating—eating and using the bin. We are eating while using the bin. Life is glorious. We want to live forever. We want to eat forever.

JANUARY 24, 1945

Cipi, Cipi, where are you? You were marching next to me. You saw me run when I saw Rachel run. Rachel ran only because she saw Chicha run. I ran only because I saw Rachel run. Rachel and I were certainly not thinking. Chicha must have been. She was the one to notice that the SS men had gone to the rear. She was on the outside of the column. Her act, I feel, was more than just instinct. It was a sudden flash of evaluation, of assessing the situation. It was a moment that called for crystal-clear thinking. And she was capable of it. We merely followed.

Cipi, how could you not have followed? How could you not? Were you not the one who said that no matter in what shape—legless, armless—you want to survive, we all must survive? You said that over and over again. What became of your will to live? Were you afraid that we would be caught? Were you so paralyzed by fear that you could only march ahead with the devil? Did their intimidation eat into your soul that deeply? I cannot understand.

For all these many years I have tried to grapple with this awesome riddle, and I cannot come to terms with it. You were supposed to follow us blindly because our instincts were the direct opposite of theirs—therefore, what we did had to be right. They chewed up your soul. They chewed it up and I was left crying. Had I known, I would have pulled you along. Was I supposed to pull you? Was I supposed to tug at your ragged sleeve? Was I?

Then, much later, others who saw you, and lived to tell, spoke your words: "My sisters, they have escaped. They will live. May the gods be with them and help them every step of the way!"

They told us how, on your way to Bergen-Belsen, you made several attempts to escape, how your proud spirit reasserted itself. But it was too late, and you were caught.

They told us how you begged the murderers to kill you, but they wouldn't because they knew you had lost your sisters to freedom, and to be alone is more agonizing than a bullet.

They told us how your agony drew smiles to their foul lips, and how they dragged you for three long weeks on the death march to Bergen-Belsen.

And they told us that you still lived when the British liberated Bergen-Belsen. But then you lived no more.

Cipi!

JANUARY 24, 1945–EVENING

We dare not go out during the day. It is evening now. There is a chicken in captivity in the yard. We must eat that too. Rachel steps out to get the chicken. She doesn't know how to kill it, so she slams it against the wall and reappears with the prize.

Chicken soup—no matter where, no matter how—is a cure for everything. That is the old adage, and it works. Our spirits soar at the smell of it. My mother would be happy.

Suddenly, the lights go out. Chicha says the Germans must have evacuated the town. They have cut the power.

The dreamer dreams. The rest of us are skeptical, laughing at her dreams. We are feasting on the last supper.

RACHEL, I SALUTE YOU

You were so vulnerable, so terrified of being separated. The terror kept you awake in Auschwitz more than the rest of us. You barely slept. Our hearts were weeping for you more than for any of us.

But, Rachel, when we couldn't, you killed the chicken for us to eat. And though you were unable to kill the memory of the madman, you were alive and well when he killed himself. And if loyalty can be fierce, you are fierce. You killed the chicken, and you would have killed anything in sight for your sisters. You were the little mother to us, forever going to Prauschnitz to organize, to find food and clothing for us after we were liberated.

And later, on our way to America, you were the mother hen, sitting on the deck of the ship, cutting up a blanket to sew into a coat for me because I was cold. The endless care. The endless concern. Our complete confidence that we could rely on you. We always blessed you. Did you know that?

But above all, in spite of your premonitions, in spite of your fear of separation, in spite of your words "Do not count on me to stay alive," in spite of your self—your life force, the landscape of your spirit, was greater than all of your words, and you remained alive.

So now, Rachel, I salute you.

JANUARY 25, 1945

And we eat and eat and eat. There is an orgy of smoked pig, but not a crust of bread to go with it. All that grease and fat without bread is murder on our stomachs, but the cycle of eating and shitting does not stop. Is there food enough on this planet to satiate the remnants of Auschwitz? It does not seem so. Eat, shit, and back to bed under the warm down covers.

We are all in bed, resting between the heavy chores of eating, emptying our sickly stomachs, and waiting for liberation or death. Suddenly the door opens, and a short man with a huge mustache is standing there. He is wearing civilian clothes and is unarmed.

Is he the last man we will ever see? Who is he? "I advise you to leave," says the man. "The Germans are all around. They'll soon discover you and kill you. Leave."

"We have no place to go," we reply. "Where should we go? . . . Is there no chance to be liberated? . . . Is it this house you want? . . . The contents? . . . We don't want the house. . . . We just want to eat and rest. . . . Let us stay. . . . Don't frighten us anymore. . . . Leave us in peace, to live or to die."

The man, a Pole brought to Germany with so many others after the *Blitzkrieg*, vanishes and leaves behind a renewed feeling of terror. The time is about 11 A.M., Thursday. Back to the food. Back to bed. I am wearing a little blue cotton dress for a nightgown. I found it in one of the armoires. Some of the nightgowns worn by the others are fancy. They came from the carefully organized dowry chest left behind. Indeed, everything was left behind. Had we not been so busy eating, we could have had quite a fashion show of embroidered undies. But we had better things to do. We had to count the hours left to us.

Will the little man with the big mustache inform on us? Will he keep our existence secret? What will he do? If we start on the road, we'll surely be discovered. We must stay. It clearly is the only choice. Out there is certain death. In here, at least, there is food. Do we have any allegiance? Yes. To food. Back under the covers. Our depression is total. Our house is at the end of the road. And this, indeed, is the end of the road.

It is now 1 P.M. The deadly silence is broken sharply, suddenly. There are noises, harsh noises—of trucks, horses, tanks, war machinery of every kind. Did the whole German army come to get us? All this for six skeletons? An orgy of deadly machinery for a handful of bones?

You stupid, stupid Hitler. We haven't any guns. We couldn't possibly harm you. We don't know anything about the business of killing. You are the genius of death. We mean to give life, to cherish it, to cradle it. You, army, turn back. Your opponent doesn't know how to kill.

Carefully, terrified, the six of us tiptoe to the window. We move the curtain ever so slightly so that we may see the life snuffers making their deadly moves toward us. And there is so much to be seen. Tanks, trucks, ammunition carriers, blood-splattered soldiers, bedraggled soldiers—worn, dying, on horses, on foot, pitiful, not brave, just spent, wretched look-ing. They have no nationality, no politics, no ideology. They are just battle weary and worn. Who are they? What do they want from us? Why don't they go home and get bandaged with gauze and love? Men, you need care. Do not spend the little strength you have on killing us. Seek solace, not hate. Seek out your children. They need your love. They need to give you theirs. Stop killing. Stop it.

But wait. Wait. These men are wearing strange uniforms. They are not German or Hungarian. They are unfamiliar. And there is a red flag—red, red.

What is red?

Red is not German, red is Russian.

We are . . . we are—What? What are we? We are . . . we are . . . we are liberated!

Barefoot, wearing only a single garment each, we all surge out into the brutal January frost and snow of eastern Germany and run toward the troops. Shrieks of joy. Shrieks of pain. Shrieks of deliverance. All the pent-up hysteria accumulated over years of pain and terror suddenly released.

I have never since heard sounds like those we uttered, sounds released from the very depths of our being. The sheer force of it must have scattered the ashes of Auschwitz to every corner of the universe, for our cries of joy suddenly turned into a bitter wail: "We are liberated! We are liberated! But where are they all? They are all dead!"

THE US MERCHANT MARINE SHIP

Why can't I remember the name of the American attaché in Odessa? The man with the large heart. The man of few words. All action.

We are in Odessa. It is late in the afternoon. It has taken us four weeks of steady traveling. We started out in Jagadschutz on foot. We walked for two weeks, then found a train that moved ever so slowly. But it did get to Odessa.

All kinds of survivors are gathered here to be sent home. We, too, want to be sent home. But not to the land of hate where we were born. There is nothing awaiting us there. No one.

We must reach across the ocean. We must reach the only surviving member of our family—our father, the defeated man who was unable to save his family.

On the morning of April 5, 1945, we go to see the American attaché. We speak no English. Our translator is a British officer who speaks to us in Yiddish. The attaché promises to put us on the next ship leaving for America—within sixteen or seventeen days. "Be happy. Relax. We'll watch over you."

But the man is too moved by our appearance and our story. He heads straight for the docks to look for a ship that might be leaving sooner.

The *Brand Whitlock* is sailing the next morning.

"Captain," the attaché says, "I have a number of American soldiers [former prisoners of war] for you to take back. And four ladies—three Hungarian girls who survived Auschwitz and one German-American woman who went back to the fatherland when Hitler was, riding high. Now that his star is falling, she is returning to the States as a naturalized U.S. citizen."

That afternoon, the attaché comes to our door at the displaced persons camp and tells us that we are to leave for America the following day. He explains that since the war is not yet over, we are to sail on a U.S. Merchant Marine ship. The ship has delivered tanks to Russia and will be carrying home a human cargo of soldiers. We will be dressed in military clothes, in the smallest-size male uniforms. Unfortunately, he has no female uniforms on hand.

On the morning of April 6, 1945, the attaché drives us in his jeep to the *Brand Whitlock*, and the entire crew is on deck to greet the three little lady soldiers. The attaché wishes us well. We never see him again.

Oh, my God, what was his name?

Five weeks of floating heaven smooth the rough edges of terror just a little. We sail across half the world, and all is well except for one ugly night when I enter our quarters unnoticed by our German-American cabin companion. She is sitting on her bed and, with her precious memorabilia spread all about, kissing the stamps with Hitler's face on them.

May you suffer, wherever you are. Amen.

MY SORROW

It crossed the ocean. It was en route for five weeks and then we arrived. She and I. Like two good friends. No! Not at all. I don't like her, but she likes me. She follows me everywhere, refuses to separate from me, even though I hadn't promised to bring her along. On the contrary. But she came anyway. I pleaded with her. "Look," I said, "it's been enough. Stay behind. You've followed me incessantly, but there's a limit. There is little room. It is crowded here, and you are such a giant." As if I wasn't speaking to her at all, she followed me into my cabin. She was ugly, an intolerable travel companion. I was forever trying to leave her behind.

If she stayed and I arrived alone, everything would be different—a new human being, in a new world, starting a new life. I'll go out on the deck and dump her in the ocean, I thought. Let her swim back where she came from, Europe.

Puff, puff, choke to death, drop dead. What do I care? Mission accomplished, I was on my way back to the cabin. Suddenly, a voice within: You thought so, eh? No! No!

I am enduring her again, as I did so often. It is only forty-eight hours more. Only twenty-four. I can already see the land. I am looking forward to the new world. She keeps dragging me back. I am begging her, "Stay behind! There is a new world out there. I want to see it. I want to live. With you it is not possible. *I beg you!*"

She interrupts me. She is cold. Merciless. She tells me what I was afraid she'd say: "*I will live as long as you do.*"

When we arrived, not even the people standing next to me noticed the ugly, clumsy giant putting her arms around me.

What is a normal life span?

MIRROR

They are marching to the smell of death. Their boots are shining like mirrors reflecting the smoke that fills the earth, the heavens.

And a year later, when I am in America and my aunt pleads with me to put on some lipstick so that I might look like an American and I refuse because I don't know yet how people live, I know only how they die—not how they die in real life, in normal life, only how they are murdered by the millions—I am all confused. I come from another planet, or my aunt does.

Then I accept the little mirror handed to me, and the lipstick. And I make believe that I am here, alive, like other people. Yes, I will make my lips beautiful red, vibrant. It will look other people, and nobody will Know where I come from. If I look like everyone else, most assuredly I will feel like everyone else. I will have conquered it all.

My hands are not steady, but now I am determined. I begin to move the lipstick on my upper lip, and I look into the mirror. But all I can see is smoke . . . smoke circling madly on the mirror. I can't see what I am doing. My lips are red, huge, smeared. I am wearing the grin of a clown.

And my aunt weeps softly.

MAY

———

May is such a "big" month. The first of May has overtones of political celebrations, and that is meaningful to me. In my teens, the first of May meant serenading under your window, a burst of spring, love, music, all sentimentally shouting hosannas in your body, masking the dread of reality.

May 1st is my sister's birthday. There is something special about being born on May 1st, and dear little Rachel is special. There is something special about being born any time in May—May 1st, May 28th. The scent of spring is delicious. It permeates the air. It sings the song of birth, of life. All is drenched in sun. The earth smiles. It is happy you are here.

The world ended in May. I was born in May. I died in May. We started the journey of ugliness on May 29th. We headed for Auschwitz. We arrived on May 31st.

The scent of spring wasn't delicious. The earth didn't smile. It shrieked in pain. The air was filled with the stench of death. Unnatural death. The smoke was thick. The sun couldn't crack through. The scent was the smell of burning flesh. The burning flesh was your mother.

I am condemned to walk the earth for all my days with the stench of burning flesh in my nostrils. My nostrils are damned. May is damned. May should be abolished. May hurts. There should be only eleven months in a year. May should be set aside for tears. For six million years, to cleanse the earth.

For more than twenty years I have walked zombie-like toward the end of May, deeply depressed, losing jobs, losing lovers, uncomprehending. And then June would come, and there would be new zeal, new life.

Now I am older, and I don't remember all the pain, and June hurts, and so does May. May laughs sometimes, and so does June, and now in May I bend down to smell the flowers, and for moments I don't recall the smell of burning flesh. That is not happiness, only relief, and relief is blessed. Now I want to reinstate the month of May. I want to reincarnate the month, reincarnate the dead. I want to tell my mother that I kept her faith, that I lived because she wanted me to, that the strength she imbued me with is not for sale, that the god in man is worth living for, and I will make sure that I hand that down to those who come after me.

I will tell them to make what is good in all of us their religion, as it was yours, Mother, and then you will always be alive and the housepainter will always be dead. And children someday will plant flowers in Auschwitz, where the sun couldn't crack through the smoke of burning flesh. Mother, I will keep you alive.

PETER

Mama, Mama, I'm pregnant!

Isn't that a miracle, Mama? Isn't it incredible, Mama?

I stood in front of the crematorium, and now there is another heart beating within that very body that was condemned to ashes. Two lives in one, Mama—I'm pregnant!

Mama, we've named him Peter. You know how much I like that name. It translates into stone, or rock. You were the rock, Mama. You laid the foundation. Peter has started the birth of the new six million.

Mama, you did not die!

Mama, he weighed seven pounds, four and a half ounces. I weighed only seven times that much when the housepainter painted thick, gray streaks in the sky.

And when I gently ease the bottle between his tender lips and he is satisfied, drinking life, I too am drunk with life. But I cannot help it, Mama, I remember.

I remember the two longest nine months of my life—the nine months while I was counting the seconds to see the life within me, and the nine months while I was dazed, half-crazed, wondering whether the liberators would come in time to save a single heartbeat.

It is all crazy, Mama. Life is ebbing away in the mad pictures of my mind. Life is being nourished in my arms. Help me, Mama. Help me to see only life. Don't let me see the madman anymore.

RICHARD

Mama, Mama, the shadow of the madman is fading!

We have another son, Mama. We have named him Richard. He is like nothing else on the face of the earth. He looks like Uncle Joe and Aunt Sara, like all of our cousins, like all of our family.

He looks like nobody else.

He is the sound of your soul. He is the voice of the six million. He is Richard.

Mama, I make this vow to you: I will teach my sons to love life, to respect man, and to hate only one thing—war.

EPILOGUE

THIS TIME IN PARIS
By Irving A. Leitner

The first time Isabella and I vacationed in Europe, we had been married only four years. It was 1960, and we left Peter, our one-year-old, in upstate New York with Isabella's older sister. When we returned nearly a month later to retrieve him, he fidgeted and cried for almost an hour before accepting us back as his rightful parents. Instinctively, at the age of one, he knew how to make us feel guilty for abandoning him while we traipsed about the continent. This time, fifteen years later, we took Peter along, as well as his thirteen-year-old brother, Richard.

On that first trip, we had spent a week in Paris, a week in Rome, and ten glorious days skittering about in general—from Cannes on the Riviera to Florence, Venice, Verona, Milan, Zurich, and London. It was exciting, exhilarating, and exhausting, and we lived on the accumulated memories for a decade and a half. Pointedly, we avoided setting foot in any German city and swiftly moved out of earshot whenever we heard German spoken.

Our resolve in 1960 to avoid anything remotely German was tinged with irony, however, for as it turned out, the dearest friend we made on that trip, and the person who guided us daily around Paris, was a middle-aged German woman to whom we had carried a letter of introduction from a mutual friend in the States. But then, Madame D was an expatriate who had left her native land in revulsion during the period of Hitler's ascendancy and had worked in the French resistance movement during World War II.

Madame D walked with us endlessly and tirelessly, conversing softly in fluent English while we avidly absorbed the sights, sounds, and smells of the magnificent streets and boulevards. On our final day in the city, she took us to the old and shabby Jewish quarter, where a shrine had been erected as a memorial to those who had been systematically murdered in the Nazi extermination camps. It was late in the day, and long shadows were falling as we approached the memorial. Madame D and I slackened our pace, but Isabella quickened hers. Suddenly, Isabella broke down and wept uncontrollably. Madame D whispered, "Go to her. Comfort her." I moved swiftly to Isabella's side. The three of us stood there in the gathering darkness, forlornly contemplative—I with my arms about Isabella, Madame D a respectful distance behind. After a while, we simply turned and left.

In Venice, about ten days later, some mysterious impulse drove us once again to seek identification with our roots. We sought out the old ghetto quarter, trod the ancient streets, and walked the Rialto bridge. A vision of Shakespeare's Shylock materialized for me: *". . . many a time and oft/ In the Rialto, you have rated me/ . . . You call me misbeliever, cutthroat dog, /And spit upon my Jewish gaberdine. . . ."*

In Rome, on a Friday evening, we asked a priest to direct us to a synagogue. He looked at us with incredulity, then taken with our audacity, led us there himself. He had never visited the area, he confided in halting English, and felt it was as good a time as any to see what a synagogue looked like in the city of churches.

When we arrived, a sprinkling of elderly worshipers were standing about in front of the building. The services had not yet begun, and pleasantries were being exchanged. At the unfamiliar sight of the black-frocked priest and the alien young couple halting before their synagogue, the Roman Jews stopped talking and stared at us with suspicion.

Unable to speak Italian, we asked the priest whether he would explain to the people that we wished them no harm, that we were only visiting. But our request was more than the priest felt comfortable with. He demurred and we understood. He agreed, however, to wait for us while we peeked inside. I then covered my bare head with a raincap, and Isabella and I walked into the house of worship.

Immediately beyond the outer door, an attendant directed Isabella in Italian to a flight of stairs at the left. Evidently, this was an Orthodox synagogue, and as was customary, men worshiped separately and apart from women. Since we actually had not come to pray, only to "see," Isabella pointed to her watch and said in English, "Just a minute," and raced up the stairs while I proceeded through the doors on the ground floor.

I really don't know what we expected to see, but somehow it felt right that we should be there, even for only a minute. When Isabella met me outside a few moments later, we rejoined the priest, who was waiting patiently on the other side of the street.

"Why didn't you stay to pray?" he asked.

"We're not religious," I said. "We were just curious."

"I was impressed," said the priest. "There were more worshipers here than in many of Rome's churches. A lot of the churches are empty every Sunday."

"Most of the worshipers tonight were old," I said, as though my comment somehow explained the phenomenon.

In London and in Paris in 1975, ancient ghettos and synagogues were quite remote in our minds. Isabella and I wanted to show our sons the sights the two capitals were famous for.

We didn't want to be sophisticated. We wanted to gape and gawk and see things perhaps a bit as we remembered them. And so we did, and relished every single moment of it.

This time in Paris, however, we did not see our old German friend Madame D, who was out of town on holiday. But we did see our Turkish friend Jessica and her American husband, George, whom we had met in the States some years before. The day before we were to return to New York, we arranged to spend the afternoon visiting the ancient cemetery of Père-Lachaise, where such diverse personalities as Honoré de Balzac, Sarah Bernhardt, Oscar Wilde, and Frédéric Chopin were buried, among the tombs and bones of thousands of other mortals and immortals.

Isabella and I still had not forgotten the visit we had made to a cemetery in Florence back in 1960. It was a Saint's Day then, and the sight of processions of people carrying lighted candles and flowers, wending their way in the soft evening light through the statuary, tombs, and graves, was deeply lodged in our memories. We hoped now in Paris to recapture some of the feelings we had experienced then. We were disappointed, of course, but the visit to Père-Lachaise was not without its special moments.

As we moved along the narrow paths and lanes, we suddenly found ourselves in a relatively new section of the ancient cemetery—Jessica informed us that it was called the martyrs' area—and there, rising hauntingly from the earth, one after the other, was a series of sculptures commemorating the murdered millions of the Nazi concentration camps.

One sculpture, dedicated to the victims of Maidanek, depicted a towering flight of steps on which a child was struggling upward; another, a desolate, faceless figure, recalled the nameless horrors of Auschwitz; a third, with the names of several *Vernichtungslager* chiseled at the base, showed three skeletal figures clawing at the sky.

Until that instant, Isabella and I had managed to dwell only on the joy of our trip—time enough later for current events, current wars, current crises. For the interlude of July 1975, there was to have been no ugly past, no bitter memories—only pleasure and enrichment.

Still, there had been small, disturbing intrusions, reminders of another time, another place. Fifteen years earlier, everywhere we went we had met American tourists by the scores; now the tourists seemed to be mainly Germans or Japanese. It was almost impossible to avoid the Germans. Isabella, for the most part, tried to ignore them. "I don't mind the young ones so much," she said; "they are an innocent generation. It's the older ones . . ."

But now, in a doleful corner of Père-Lachaise, the fragile fantasy we had so carefully nourished was suddenly demolished. Yet this time, unlike 1960, there were no tears, no heart-wrenching tugs, no need for consolation. This time Isabella wanted only a photograph as a personal remembrance.

She posed briefly for Peter, and we left the cemetery, Jessica and her husband going their way, and we returning to our hotel.

Since our second day in Paris, we had made it a nightly ritual, before retiring, to spend some time in a modest café near our hotel, to relax, chat, and reconstruct the day's events. With our departure scheduled for the following noon, this was to be our last evening at the Café Cristal. The weather, which had been glorious for most of our trip, had suddenly turned dismal. A light rain was falling, casting a certain moodiness over us as we entered the glass-enclosed terrace.

The unexpected jolt at Père-Lachaise, coupled with the knowledge that our vacation was ending, had had a sobering effect upon us all. Still, we were determined to extract every last bit of experience possible and tuck it away as a joyful memory of Paris. And so we sat down and gave the waiter our orders.

Isabella had just lit one of her short French cigarettes, and four foaming cups of *café au lait* had barely been placed on our table, when all at once a group of ten or twelve tourists, both men and women, streamed through the two terrace doors and out of the rain. Amid much stamping of feet, doffing of hats and coats, and bantering remarks, the newcomers began to move the tables and chairs about so that they could all be together. The problem for them seemed to be our small table, which was centrally located against the terrace wall, preventing them from grouping all the tables on either one side or the other.

Suddenly, a feeling of dismay clutched me, for in a flash I realized that all the men and women were Germans.

"Who do you think they are?" Isabella whispered.

"Danes," I replied, in an effort to shield her from the truth. The irony of this development coming so soon upon the heels of Père-Lachaise seemed almost too much to bear.

The Germans, appearing somewhat exasperated at our presence, finally decided to divide their party into a semi-circle. Two men took a table to our left, two to our right, and the remainder shoved their tables together in the open area behind us. Isabella, with her back to the terrace wall, as well as the boys and I, felt literally surrounded.

With growing anxiety, I watched Isabella's face carefully for the first signs of recognition. She was obviously intrigued by all the fuss and commotion. As the man at her elbow glanced in our direction, a broad, red-faced grin expanding his jowls—an apparent overture of friendliness—Isabella suddenly asked, "Danish?"

"*Nein,*" replied the stranger, "*Deutsch. Von München.*"

Isabella reacted as though acid had been hurled in her face. She seemed to shrivel in her seat. She covered her eyes to blot the man out of her sight. An instant later, with head lowered and lids tightly closed, she placed her palms over her ears, trying to block out every sound.

The grin on the red-faced German vanished. With a guttural murmur and a scraping movement, he readjusted his posture. He mumbled something to his companion, and from the corner of my eye, I could see that both were irritated.

I looked at Peter and Richard. Their faces were ashen. I reached out and touched Isabella. She slowly opened her eyes. "It's them," she whispered, tears spilling down her cheeks. "It's them. They're just the right age."

"Let's get out of here," I said. "Let's go." I glanced around. Each and every German appeared to be in his or her sixties. Isabella was right. They were all "just the right age."

"Any one of them could have been my jailer—especially this one. I had a red-faced *Oberscharführer* who used to grin like that. He used to club people, and whip them, and grin like a hyena with his ugly little teeth."

"Let's go," I whispered urgently. I signaled the waiter for my check. I could sense that the Germans knew something was wrong at our table. They were exchanging half-audible remarks and glancing pointedly in our direction. I had a distinct feeling they thought Isabella was crazy.

At last the waiter brought the check. I had the money ready and stood up immediately. The boys followed suit. But Isabella could not move.

"Come on, Mommy," Peter said.

I extended my arm to help her up. She took it and rose wearily. "They're the ones," she muttered. "They're the ones."

Negotiating our way past the Germans posed a problem because they had pushed their chairs and tables so close together, but we finally made it through the terrace door and into the rain. We felt the eyes of the Germans following us all the way.

Outside, Isabella took several steps, paused, and then in a rising crescendo of pain began to scream, "Murderers! Murderers! Murderers!" Peter, Richard and I quickly hurried her off.

About twenty yards from our hotel, Isabella suddenly stopped and clutched her back. "Help me. I can't walk," she said.

The boys and I sprang to her aid to keep her from sinking to the ground. We stood there in a tight cluster without moving. Not a person passed us. The street was deserted. The rain was now falling heavily.

After what seemed an eternity, Isabella said, "I think I can make it."

We walked the final few steps to the hotel and dropped into four separate chairs in the lobby.

"Are you all right, Mommy?" Richard asked.

"I think so, darling," Isabella responded. "I think so." Then turning to me, she repeated, "They're the ones. There's no doubt about it. They're the ones."

"How can you be so sure?" I asked.

"Did you see that man's face when he said, 'Von München'— the pride, the gleam in his eyes? He was no Madame D. He never left Germany. He's the typical *'Deutschland über alles'* German, the Nazi murderer. He could be the one who killed my mother."

"You have no proof," I said.

"I don't need any proof. He's from that generation—the Hitler generation. Have you ever heard a German say he knew about the camps? No. And yet they had to know. When I was in Birnbaumel, they used to march us skeletons through the streets every morning and every night to dig tank traps against the Russians. Twice a day the people saw us. Every day. And if you asked them now, not a one would admit it. And this took place in cities and towns all over Germany. Why, the smoke from the crematoriums blew over their homes twenty-four hours a day. The stench alone should have told them what was going on."

"We've got to do something," Peter suddenly said. "We just can't leave it like this. It's too frustrating."

"We can't ever escape them," Isabella said. "Not until that whole generation has died out."

"I'm going to write them a note," Peter said, taking a small pad and a pen from his pocket.

"What kind of note?"

"I don't know—just a note—just something to make them feel guilty." He thought for a moment, and then, in small block letters, he printed three short lines:

Auschwitz

Bergen-Belsen

Dachau

"Good," I said. "If they had anything to do with the camps, this will tell them they were recognized. If they were innocent, it will explain why we left."

"How are you going to deliver it?" Isabella asked.

"I'd like to throw it in their faces," Peter said.

The boys and I rose and headed for the door.

"I'm staying here," Isabella said, "so please hurry back. I'll be worried. . . ."

The rain, which had been falling so heavily only a few moments before, had now tapered off to a misty drizzle. The wet terrace windows of the café glistened with shimmering light as we approached. The Germans were still all there. We could see them laughing. Clearly, they were enjoying their Parisian holiday. It made me doubly angry because they had so marred ours.

At the corner, we stopped and watched them from directly across the street. There suddenly seemed to be so many of them—*a whole Nazi army*.

"I don't think I can do it," Peter said haltingly.

"Do you think we should, Dad?" Richard asked.

"Give me the note," I said.

"How are you going to do it?" Peter asked as he handed me the paper.

I didn't answer directly. I was still undecided about how to proceed but determined that the message be delivered. I folded the note and started across the street. The boys stood in the drizzle and watched me. "Be careful, Dad," I heard Richard say.

As I entered the café, the throaty sounds of German speech assailed my ears. I stepped across the terrace and into the café proper. A semicircular bar confronted me. A lone cashier was standing at a register totaling the day's receipts. On the bar, a small stack of metal trays, the ones the waiters used to carry the checks to diners, caught my eye. I walked to the bar and took a tray from the stack. I placed the note on the tray and returned to the terrace. For a brief moment, I hesitated as the Germans looked up at me. Then, without a word, and as discreetly as a waiter presenting a check, I set the tray before the Germans at the table closest to me. As one of them reached for the note, I casually stepped out the terrace door and walked back to my children.

IMAGE GALLERY

Isabella in her twenties.

Isabella and her family in Kisvárda, Hungary, shortly before deportation in 1944. Back row (left to right): Chicha, Isabella, Philip, Cipi, Rachel. Front row (left to right): Potyo and their mother, Teresa.

Isabella in New York City in the early 1950s.

Isabella at film director Sam Spiegel's office in New York City
where she worked in 1955.

Isabella and Irving married in New York City in 1956.

Isabella in Manhattan's Greenwich Village in the 1950s
with her award-winning sculpture of her mother as Isabella
remembered her.

Isabella holding her firstborn, Peter,
in New York City in 1960.

Isabella with her two sons, Peter and Richard,
in New York City in 1967.

Chicha, Isabella, Rachel, and Phillip in
New York City in the 1970s.

Isabella with her husband, Irving, in the 1970s.

ABOUT THE AUTHOR

Isabella Leitner (1921–2009) was born and raised in Hungary. On her twenty-third birthday, she was deported to Auschwitz along with her mother, four sisters, and brother, an experience she wrote about in her acclaimed memoir *Fragments of Isabella*, which was published in 1978 and named an American Library Association Best Book for Young Adults. A motion picture based on the book was produced by the Abbey Theater in Ireland and a theatrical play adapted from the book by Irving A. Leitner premiered in 1993 in St. Petersburg, Russia, to commemorate the forty-eighth anniversary of the end of World War II. In 1945, the author immigrated to the United States and married Irving A. Leitner, who served in a US Air Force bomber squadron during World War II. The mother of two sons, Peter and Richard, whom she considered "her greatest victory over Hitler," Leitner also wrote *Saving the Fragments: From Auschwitz to New York and The Big Lie: A True Story.*

OPEN  ROAD

INTEGRATED MEDIA

CPSIA information can be obtained
at www.ICGtesting.com
Printed in the USA
LVHW091543201121
703958LV00004B/294